John Rutter

Carols

10 carols for mixed voices

Contents

MUSIC DEPARTMENT

OXFORD
UNIVERSITY PRESS

OXFORD
UNIVERSITY PRESS

Great Clarendon Street, Oxford OX2 6DP, England

Oxford University Press is a department of the University of Oxford.
It furthers the University's aim of excellence in research, scholarship,
and education by publishing worldwide

Oxford is a registered trade mark of Oxford University Press
in the UK and in certain other countries

16

ISBN 978-0-19-353381-3

Music originated on Sibelius
Printed in Great Britain on acid-free paper by
Halstan & Co. Ltd., Amersham, Bucks.

Cover photograph of John Rutter © Ian Cole

Index of Orchestrations

The accompanied items are all available in versions with orchestra. Full scores and instrumental parts are available on hire from the publisher, and also on sale where shown. In the USA some items are available from Hinshaw Music, Inc. Details of instrumentation are shown below.

Angels' Carol
2fl, ob, 2cl, bsn, 2hn, hp, str (*hire*)
In USA: available on sale from Hinshaw Music, Inc.

Candlelight Carol
fl, ob, hp, str (*hire*)
In USA: available on sale from Hinshaw Music, Inc.

Dormi, Jesu
strings (*hire*)
In USA: available on sale from Hinshaw Music, Inc.

Love came down at Christmas
strings (*hire*)

Mary's Lullaby
fl, ob, hp, str (*hire and sale*)

Nativity Carol
strings (and organ *ad lib.*) (*hire and sale*)

Shepherd's Pipe Carol
fl/picc, ob, bsn, 2hn, hp (opt), str (*hire and sale*)

Star Carol
2fl, 2ob, 2cl, 2bsn, 2hn, 2perc, hp, str (*hire and sale*)
Also available with brass accompaniment: 4tpt, 3tbn, tuba, timp, perc, piano or organ (*hire*)

What sweeter music
strings (*hire and sale*)

Hinshaw Music, Inc.: www.hinshawmusic.com

Angels' Carol

Words and music by
JOHN RUTTER

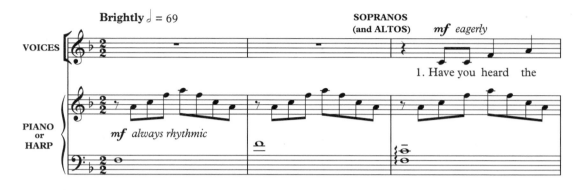

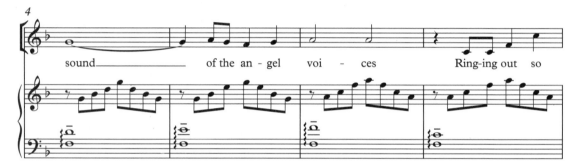

Also available separately (X325), and in a two-part version for upper voices (T117). In the USA, this four-part version is available separately from Hinshaw Music, Inc. (HMC1002); the two-part version is also available separately (HMC986).

Glo-ri-a in ex-cel-sis De-o! Hear the an-gels sing their joy-ful

Glo-ri-a in ex-cel-sis De-o! Hear them sing their joy-ful

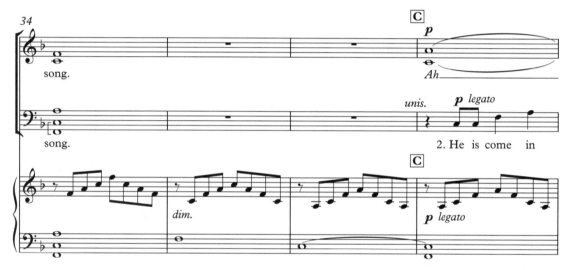

song. Ah

song. 2. He is come in

peace in the win-ter's still-ness, Like a gen-tle

Ah

love_____ as the child of Ma - ry; In a sim - ple

Hum

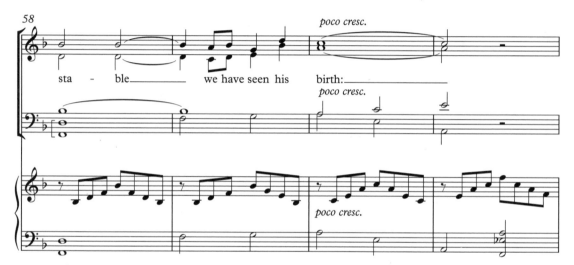

sta - ble_____ we have seen his birth:_____

poco cresc.

Glo-ri - a in ex - cel - sis De - o!

Glo-ri - a in ex - cel - sis De - o,

for John Romeri and the Church of the Assumption, Pittsburgh

Candlelight Carol

Words and music by
JOHN RUTTER

Also available separately (X292) and in a version for SSAA (W104). In the USA this mixed-voice version is available separately from Hinshaw Music, Inc. (HMC798); also available separately for SSAA (HMC894).

*or hum, at conductor's discretion

for Stephen Cleobury and the choir of King's College, Cambridge

Dormi, Jesu

Words: Latin, origin unknown
English, S. T. Coleridge (1772–1834)

JOHN RUTTER

Also available separately (X433). In the USA, this carol is available separately from Hinshaw Music, Inc. (HMC1718).

24

Love came down at Christmas

Words by
Christina Rossetti (1830–94)

JOHN RUTTER

This carol may be performed in G flat major. Also available separately, in G flat major (X224).

for JoAnne

Mary's Lullaby

Words and music by
JOHN RUTTER

Also available separately (X272), and in a version for SSA (W111).

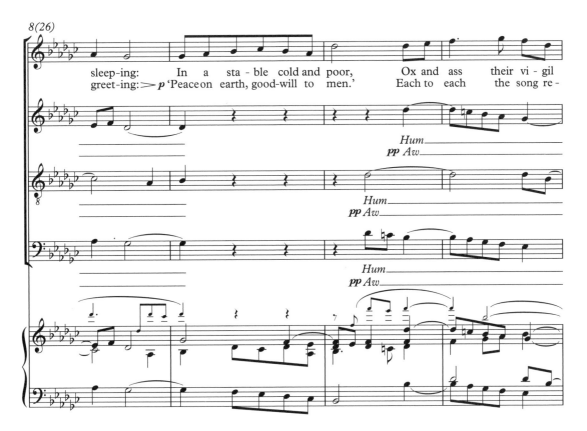

Nativity Carol

Words and music by
JOHN RUTTER

Also available separately (X169), and for unison voices (U154). A version for upper voices, SSA, is included in *Carols for Choirs 4*.

34

Shepherd's Pipe Carol

Words and music by
JOHN RUTTER

Also available separately (X167), and in versions for SSAA (W76), and for unison voices (U133).

cra - dled there at Beth - le - hem.'

3. 'None may hear my pipes on these hills so lone - ly

Ah

Ah

Ah

where the babe was ly-ing cra-dled in the arms of his mo-ther Ma - ry,

Ah

Ah

Ah

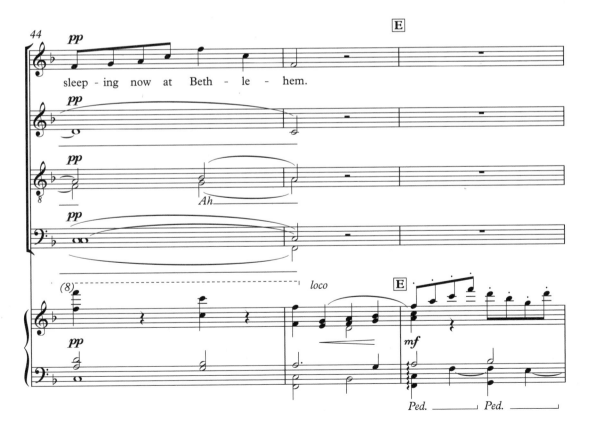

sleep-ing now at Beth - le - hem.

Ah

TENORS and BASSES *mf crisply*

4. 'Where is this new King, shep-herd boy pi-ping mer-ri-ly,

Is he there at Beth - le - hem?'_ 'I will find him soon by the

star shi-ning bright - ly In the sky o'er Beth - le - hem.'_

5. 'May I come with you, shep-herd boy pi-ping mer-ri-ly, Come with you to Beth - le - hem?_

Pay my hom-age too at the new King's cra - dle,

Is it far to Beth - le - hem?'

An - gels in_ the sky
An - gels_

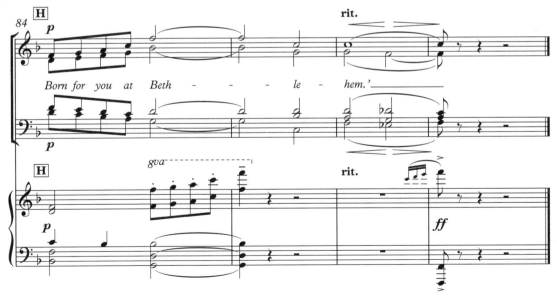

for Sir David Willcocks and The Bach Choir

Star Carol

Words and music by
JOHN RUTTER

Also available separately (X233), and in a version for unison voices (U153).

*Children and/or audience may join in the melody of the refrain, which can be taught at the time of the performance.

21 (42)

mf lightly

Hur - ry to Beth - le - hem__ and see the son__ of Ma - ry!

mf lightly

mf

2nd time only

p

24 **B**

1. 2.

mf

tr

p dolce

47 **C** *p dolce e legato*

S.

3. See, he lies in his mo - ther's ten - der keep - ing; Je - sus Christ in her

A.

p dolce e legato

*Ah

T.

p dolce e legato

*Ah

B.

p dolce e legato

*Ah

Ah

C

*or hum, at conductor's discretion

joy - ful - ly;—— Hur - ry to Beth - le - hem—— and see the son—— of Ma —— ry!

E _f_

4. Let us all pay our hom-age at the man - ger,

Sing his praise on this joy - ful Christ-mas Night; Christ is come, bring - ing

pro -mise of sal - va - tion; Hur - ry to Beth - le - hem___ and see the son___ of

Ma - ry! See his star shin - ing bright

In the sky this___ Christ - mas Night! Fol - low me joy - ful - ly;

Hur - ry to Beth - le - hem___ and see the son___ of Ma - ry,

Poco largamente   rall.

Hur - ry to Beth - le - hem___ and see the son___ of Ma - ry!___

Hur - ry to Beth - le - hem___ and see the son___ of Ma - ry!___

for Dr George Guest and the choir of St John's College, Cambridge

There is a flower

Words by
John Audelay (15th century)

JOHN RUTTER

*Alternatively, these three bars may be sung by 2nd altos.

Also available separately (X295)

54

*sand = gift
†Alternatively, the choir 1 part may be sung by solo tenor in verse 2 and solo soprano in verse 3.

*bed = bud

for Stephen Cleobury and
the choir of King's College, Cambridge

What sweeter music

*Words by
Robert Herrick
(1591–1674)

JOHN RUTTER

**Slightly abridged and altered

Also available separately (X319)

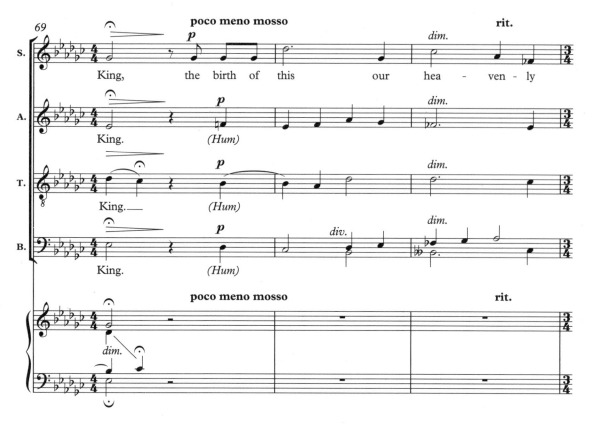

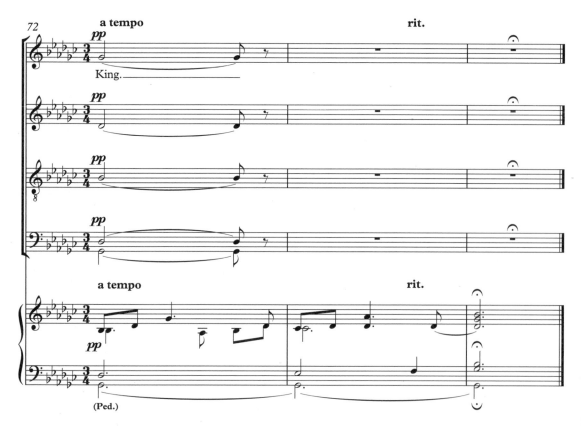